All About TEXAS

100+ Amazing & Interesting Facts

By Bandana Ojha

Introduction

Filled with up-to-date information, color photos, fascinating & fun facts this book "All About TEXAS: 100+ Amazing Facts with Pictures" is the best book for kids to find out more about the Lone Star State. This book would satisfy the children's curiosity and help them to understand why TEXAS is special—and what makes it different from other States. This book gives a story, history, the state symbols & explores the most interesting and amazing fun facts about Texas. This is a great chance for every kid to expand their knowledge about the 2nd most populous state of US and impress family and friends with all discovered and never known before amazing fun facts.

1. In December 29, 1845, the Republic of Texas was annexed to the United States of America, becoming the 28th U.S. state.

2. Texas is the second largest U.S. state by area (after Alaska) and population (after California).

3. Texas is twice the size of Germany and Japan.

4. Spain was the first European country to claim and control the area of Texas.

5. Alvar de Pineda, a Spanish explorer was the first ever European to enter in Texas in1528.

6. Texas is bordered by New Mexico in the northwest; Oklahoma in the north and northeast; Arkansas, Louisiana, and the Gulf

of Mexico in the east; and Mexico in the southwest.

7. The population of Texas is estimated to be about 29.90 million in 2020.

8. The State Abbreviation of Texas is "TX".

9. The State follows CST (Central Standard Time).

10. Name for resident of Texas is Texan.

11. The flag of Texas is the official flag of the U.S. state of Texas. It is well known for its prominent single white star which gives the flag its commonly used name: "Lone Star Flag."

12. The State seal is the "Seal of Texas"

13. The State nick name is "The Lone Star State".

14. Texas is nicknamed the Lone Star State because in 1836, when the Republic of Texas declared itself an independent nation, it flew a flag with a single star on it.

15. Texas has the second tallest state capitol building, after Louisiana.

16. The State Capital is Austin.

17. The Texas state capitol building completed on May 16, 1888, is the largest capitol of all state capitols in the nation in terms of gross square footage.

18. It is second in total size only to the National Capital in D.C. Additionally, the capitol dome in Austin is 7 feet higher than the dome on the U.S. capitol.

19. "Texas, Our Texas," is the official state song of Texas.

20. It was adopted by the Legislature in 1929 after being selected in a state-wide competition.

21. It was composed by William J. Marsh. The lyrics were written by Marsh and Gladys Yoakum Wright.

22. The state motto of Texas is "Friendship." The word, Texas, or Tejas, was the Spanish pronunciation of a Caddo Indian word meaning "friends" or "allies."

23. The state slogan is "The Friendly State".

24. The state Flower of Texas is Bluebonnets.

25. The state fruit is Texas red grapefruit.

26. The state tree is Pecan.

27. The state plant is Prickly pear cactus.

28. The state shrub is Crape myrtle

29. The state grass is Sideoats grama

30. The state bird is Northern mockingbird.

31. The state mammal(small) is Nine-banded armadillo.

32. The state mammal(large) is Texas Longhorn.

33. The state mammal(flying) is Mexican free-tailed bat.

34. The state dog is Blue Lacy

35. The state fish is Guadalupe bass.

36. The State insect is Monarch butterfly.

37. The state Gemstone is Texas blue topaz.
38. The state Fiber and fabric is cotton.

39. The state soil is Houston Black.

40. The state Musical instrument is Acoustic guitar.

41. The state stone is Petrified palmwood.

42. The state Music is Western swing.

43. The state nut is Native Pecan.

44. The state snack is Tortilla chips and salsa.

45. The state sport is Rodeo.

46. The state Vegetable is Texas sweet onion.

47. The State Pepper is Jalapeno.

48. The state Reptile is Texas horned lizard.

49. The state Folk dance is Square dance.

50. The state dish is Chili.

51. The state dinosaur is Sauroposeidon.

52. Guadalupe Peak is the highest point of Texas.

53. Gulf of Mexico is the lowest point of Texas.

54. Texas is the second most populous state in the U.S., after California.

55. Florida is the 3rd and New York is 4th most populous states of United States.

56. Texas has 254 counties which is the greatest than any other American State.

57. The state was an independent nation from 1836 to 1845.

58. Texas possesses three top ten most populous cities in the United States. These cities are Houston, Dallas, and San Antonio.

59. A wide range of animals and insects live in Texas. It is the home to 65 species of mammals, 213 species of reptiles and amphibians, and 590 species of birds.

60. Texas has 730 airports, second most of any state in the United States.

61. The Dallas/Fort Worth International Airport (DFW) is home to the world's largest parking lot.

62. Dallas/Fort Worth International Airport (DFW) is the second largest by area in the United States, and fourth in the world.

63. Denver International Airport (DIA) is the largest airport in the US.

64. In traffic, DFW is the busiest in the state, the fourth busiest in the United States, and sixth worldwide.

65. Texas's second largest airport is Houston's George Bush Intercontinental Airport (IAH).

66. The Rick Husband Amarillo International Airport has the third largest runway in the world and is the alternate landing site for the space shuttle.

67. Six flags have flown over Texas: British, French, Mexican, Texan, United States, and Confederate. That is how Six Flags amusement park got its name.

68. The first Texas freeway was the Gulf Freeway opened in 1948 in Houston.

69. Texans have historically had difficulties traversing Texas due to the state's large size and rough terrain.

70. Texas has compensated by building both America's largest highway and railway systems in length.

71. Texas has the headquarters of many high technology companies, such as Dell, Inc., Texas Instruments, Perot Systems, Rackspace and AT&T.

72. Austin is nicknamed as "Silicon Hills" and the north Dallas is nicknamed as "Silicon Prairie".

73. Texas has the most farms and the highest acreage in the United States.

74. Texas is ranked no.1 for revenue generated from total livestock and livestock products.

75. It is ranked no. 2 for total agricultural revenue, behind California.

76. The world's first rodeo was held in Pecos on July 4, 1883.

77. The annual Houston Livestock Show and Rodeo is the largest rodeo in the world.

78. Texas has the first domed stadium in the country. The structure was built in Houston and opened in April 1965.

79. The first suspension bridge in the United States was the Waco Bridge. Built in 1870 and still in use today as a pedestrian crossing of the Brazos River.

80. There are 3,700 streams and 15 big rivers in Texas.

81. Rio Grande is the largest river in Texas.

82. The state has 115 national parks.

83. The largest city in Texas is Houston. It is also the fourth largest city in the United States.

84. The King Ranch in Texas is bigger than the state of Rhode Island.

85. More land is farmed in Texas than in any other state.

86. Nationally, the Dallas–Fort Worth area, home to the second shopping mall in the United States, has the most shopping malls per capita of any American metropolitan area.

87. The Texas Medical Center in Houston holds the world's largest concentration of research and healthcare institutions, with 47 member institutions.

88. Texas Medical Center performs the most heart transplants in the world.

89. Texas leads the nation in the production of cattle, horses, sheep, goats, wool, mohair and hay.

90. Texas leads the nation in production of cotton which is the number one crop grown in the state in terms of value.

91. Edwards Plateau in west central Texas is the top sheep growing area in the country.

92. Texas is the biggest oil producer in the United States.

93. Austin is considered the live music capital of the world.

94. The National Aeronautics and Space Administration's Lyndon B. Johnson Space Center (NASA JSC) located in Southeast Houston, Texas.

95. It is home to the nation's astronaut corps, the International Space Station mission operations, the Orion Program, and a host of future space developments. The center plays a pivotal role in enhancing scientific and technological knowledge to benefit all of humankind.

96. Brazoria County is known as a bird watchers paradise, boasting approximately 400 observable species of birds.

97. Rainbow Bridge is the tallest bridge in Texas.

98. Athens, Texas claims to be the official birthplace of the American hamburger.

99. The highest temperature ever recorded in Texas was 120° F in Seymour on August 12, 1936.

100.   The lowest temperature ever recorded was -23° F at Tulia in 1899 and at Seminole on February 8, 1933.

101.   More tornados have been recorded in Texas than any other state.

102.   Two United States Presidents were born in Texas, Lyndon Johnson, and Dwight Eisenhower.

103.   The world's largest statue of an American is of Sam Houston, called a "Tribute to Courage" and is in Huntsville.

104. The Katy Freeway at Beltway 8 is the world's widest freeway at 26 lanes across.

105. San Antonio's Bracken Cave is home to the world's largest bat colony.

106.   Texas emits more greenhouse gases than any other state in the United States. If Texas were a country, it would rank as the world's 7th largest producer of greenhouse gases.

107.   The largest county in Texas is Brewster. It measures 6,193 square miles, which is roughly the size of Connecticut and 3 times size of Delaware.

108.   Texas experiences the most tornadoes in the United States, with an average of 139 per year. Tornadoes occur most often in North Texas and the Panhandle.

Please check this out:

Our other best-selling books for kids are-

All About Arizona: 100+ Amazing Fun Facts with Pictures

All About California: 100+ Amazing Fun Facts with Pictures

All About New York: 100+ Amazing Fun Facts with Pictures

All About New Jersey: 100+ Amazing Fun Facts with Pictures

All About Massachusetts: 100+ Amazing Fun Facts with Pictures

All About Italy: 100+ Amazing Fun Facts with Pictures

Know about Sharks: 100 Amazing Fun Facts with Pictures

Know About Whales:100+ Amazing & Interesting Fun Facts with Pictures: " Never known Before Whales facts"

Know About Dinosaurs: 100 Amazing & Interesting Fun Facts with Pictures

Know About Kangaroos: Amazing & Interesting Facts with Pictures

Know About Penguins: 100+ Amazing Penguin Facts with Pictures

Know About Dolphins :100 Amazing Dolphin Facts with Pictures

100 Amazing Quiz Q & A About Penguin: Never Known Before Penguin Facts

Most Popular Animal Quiz book for Kids: 100 amazing animal facts

Quiz Book for Kids: Science, History, Geography, Biology, Computer & Information Technology

English Grammar for Kids: Most Easy Way to learn English Grammar

Solar System & Space Science- Quiz for Kids: What You Know About Solar System

English Grammar Practice Book for elementary kids: 1000+ Practice Questions with Answers

A to Z of English Tense